The Common Core Readiness Guide to Reading™

TIPS & TRICKS FOR
COMPARING AND
CONTRASTING TEXTS

Sandra K. Athans and Robin W. Parente

ROSEN
PUBLISHING®

New York

Published in 2015 by The Rosen Publishing Group, Inc.
29 East 21st Street, New York, NY 10010

First Edition

Library of Congress Cataloging-in-Publication Data

Athans, Sandra K., 1958–
Tips & tricks for comparing and contrasting texts/Sandra K. Athans and Robin W. Parente.—First Edition.
    pages cm.—(The Common Core Readiness Guide to Reading)
Audience: Grade level for this book is grades 5–8.
Includes bibliographical references and index.
ISBN 978-1-4777-7543-1 (library bound)—ISBN 978-1-4777-7545-5 (pbk.)—
ISBN 978-1-4777-7546-2 (6-pack)
1. Reading comprehension—Study and teaching (Middle school) 2. Critical thinking—Study and teaching (Middle school) 3. Reading (Secondary) 4. Reader-response criticism—Study and teaching (Middle school) 5. Reading—Language experience approach. I. Parente, Robin W. II. Title. III. Title: Tips and tricks for comparing and contrasting texts.
LB1050.45.A84 2014
428.4071'2—dc23

                                                    2014004238

Manufactured in the United States of America

Contents

Introduction

So powerful

four minutes.

father left h

hool.

The Common Core Reading Standards are a set of skills designed to prepare you for entering college or beginning your career. They're grouped into broad College and Career Readiness Anchor Standards, and they help you use reasoning and evidence in ways that will serve you well now and in the future.

The skills build from kindergarten to the twelfth grade. Grades six through eight take the spotlight here. You may have already noticed changes in your classrooms that are based on the standards—deeper-level reading, shorter passages, an emphasis on informational texts, or an overall increase in rigor within your daily activities.

This book will help you understand, practice, and independently apply the skills through easy-to-use "tips and tricks." Gaining mastery of the skills is the goal.

Your teachers may use "close reading" for some of their instruction. During close reading, you read shorter passages more deeply and analytically. Close reading passages often have rich, complex content. They contain grade-level vocabulary words, sentence structures, and literary

In addition to reading within the English language arts (ELA), the standards also set requirements for literacy in history/social studies, science, and technical subjects.

techniques. Reading a short, three-page passage closely could take two to three days or more. The benefit to you is that you get a deeper, more valuable understanding of what you've read. Close reading is a critical part of the new Common Core Reading Standards and is used throughout this book.

Other well-known reading comprehension skills remain valuable. Visualizing, asking questions, synthesizing, and other traditional strategies work well together with the Common Core skills covered here.

This book focuses on Anchor Standard 9: Analyze "how two or more texts address similar themes or topics in order to build knowledge or to compare the approaches the authors take." In the next section, we'll break this standard apart and look closely at the skills of comparing and contrasting texts. Also, the tips and tricks that can help you gain mastery of this standard are introduced. Some feature visual icons that will be used throughout this book.

In the passages that follow, you tag along with expert readers as they think aloud while close reading from different passages of literature (fiction) and informational text (nonfiction). Visual icons that represent the tips and tricks appear in the margins and prompt the expert reader. Ways in which the expert reader applies them appear in "Expert Reader" margin notes. You'll also observe how the expert readers respond to multiple-choice questions, complete graphic organizers, and prepare written responses that demonstrate their comparative analysis of multiple texts.

After you gain an understanding of how the skills are applied, it's your turn to try with guided practice. You'll apply the skills independently and perform a self-evaluation by checking your responses against answers provided. Based on your responses, you can determine if another pass through the expert reader's examples might be helpful—or if you've mastered the skill.

CHAPTER 1

A QUICK AND EASY OVERVIEW: THE SKILLS AND THE TIPS & TRICKS

Let's examine the skills involved with comparing and contrasting texts. We know the words "compare" and "contrast" are verbs, something we actively do. To compare means to detect similarities among items. To contrast means to note differences among them. Mastering the analytical skills of detecting and evaluating significant similarities and differences among ideas presented in two or more texts helps you build knowledge.

As you compare and contrast texts, you may need to make inferences about ideas or events not explicitly stated. An inference is a conclusion you make by interpreting clues provided in the passage; it's as if you're reading between the lines. Your inferences must be reasonably based on something concrete in the text.

In this standard, you will be comparing and contrasting critical ways in which two texts treat a similar theme, topic, time, place, character, event, or other component. You might also analyze how different authors shape presentations on the same topic. Careful analysis of similarities and differences helps us build and integrate new knowledge into our understandings.

There may be differences in the way in which a standard is applied to literature and informational text. Continued practice with both types of genres will help build skills in addressing these differences.

These skills are useful as you read literature and informational texts, and in reading within history/social studies, science, and technical subjects. They're also useful for many of your daily, real-life activities. As you shall see, there are mild nuances in the manner in which you apply these skills to the different genres. Yet, with practice, these adjustments become automatic.

As you progress in grade levels, you're expected to conduct this type of comparative analysis across genres and among different types of texts, and explore variety among authors' presentations.

Tips & Tricks

There are several easy-to-use tips and tricks that can help you detect and explore similarities and differences among texts. Some are useful as you begin to read, while others guide you throughout your reading. Here's a quick overview of them. The icons featured below are used in subsequent sections to show you how the tips and tricks are used in action with literature and informational texts.

 ● **Launching "Jump-Start" Clues:** Before you dive into reading a piece of text, skim it. Notice and take a visual inventory of everything you see. The title, subheadings, boldface print, and other features like photographs or charts will give you valuable clues about the content and genre. Authors select and use text features purposefully. It's often helpful to ask yourself, "What could the title mean?" or "What purpose do the special features serve?" As you prepare to analyze two or more texts, jump-starting your insights by detecting the content and genre of each passage marks a good beginning.

 ● **Breaking Apart Literary Elements:** In works of literature, breaking apart and analyzing the literary elements separately is often helpful. The characters, events, and setting of a story are among the literary elements that an author carefully crafts together to move the plot forward. Determining how these elements develop and interact within the passage helps us build richer, more meaningful understandings of the story. Also, we may begin to gain an appreciation for an author's style.

Elements found within informational text can also be broken apart for analysis. Here, authors may use examples, anecdotes, comparisons, analogies, or other methods to establish relationships between individuals, events, and ideas. Considering how an author has launched and developed information is key. Also keep in mind that authors of informational text have a point to make about a topic. They frequently want to shape your thinking and will use expository, procedural, or persuasive formats.

● **Using Text Structure (Flexibly) to Find Central Ideas and Themes and to Monitor Development:** Central ideas and themes may emerge early on and then develop throughout the passage. Determining what a passage is *mostly* about will help guide you to identify central ideas and themes—which may or may not be stated explicitly in the text. Gauge the volume of coverage or "weight" given to ideas, topics, or events. This usually equates to the value an author places on specific content.

You already know a lot about the different text structures. For example, in works of fiction, characters and a setting are introduced, a problem is identified, and events lead to a solution or improvement. With these works, it's helpful to consider how the character changes from the beginning to the end of the story. Ask yourself, "What lesson does the character learn?" Noting this change or others can help you refine your ideas about theme.

With informational text, authors organize ideas in sequential, cause-and-effect, or other structures that help readers grasp and remember important information. Identifying these structures can help guide and validate your ideas about central ideas. You might ask yourself, "Has the author linked ideas together using a cause-and-effect structure?" Also, authors of information texts carefully organize information into paragraphs. Sometimes central ideas are expressed in topic or concluding sentences. Reviewing the paragraph structure can also help you spot central ideas.

● **Be Attentive to the Author:** It's important to detect what the author is saying in works of literature and in informational texts. All text is filtered through the author's perspective. Knowing this is important as you determine critical ideas that he or she is presenting. It's helpful to ask yourself, "What point, issue, or view has the author stressed?"

● **Tune in to Your Inside Voice:** Your mind is actively making sense as you read. Listening to your thoughts or your mind's "dialogue" helps you grasp meaning. Connecting new ideas to known ideas is the way your mind builds cohesive meaning. Monitoring your thoughts, including your questions, is critical: Do characters' motives, events in the story, and/or ideas seem unusual or out of place? How do charts, tables, or other special features included within a passage build your understanding? Are your reactions likely what the author intended?

In addition to helping you decipher the meaning of texts, listening to your inside voice can help guide your analysis of multiple texts. Tuning in can help you detect and explore critical similarities and differences by helping you:

1) Distinguish critical from noncritical points of analysis. Do the features you're comparing and contrasting help build or refine your understanding? Have you avoided obvious or superficial features that do not support a deeper level of understanding?

2) Make sure the content of your passages steers you in a direction of a credible analysis. Are the critical points you've identified covered adequately in each passage to make your analysis credible? Be sure you have evidence to support your views as you compare and contrast features within your texts.

3) Make sure you analyze parallel ideas between texts. Have you compared and contrasted like topics within the passages? Have you compared apples to apples and oranges to oranges? In other words, have you compared tone to tone, structure to structure, and character trait to character trait? Be sure you haven't been sidetracked and mismatched your points of analysis.

 ● **Avoid Common Pitfalls:** Sometimes we can become distracted by something in the text, which could steer us away from an author's intended meaning. Staying engaged and focused while ensuring that your ideas square with text-based evidence is critical. It's sometimes helpful to validate your interpretation by considering how you complete the following sentence: "I know this because…" Your response must be found within the passage.

As you compare and contrast multiple texts, you will also want to ensure you have avoided analyzing elements that are inconsequential in terms of building your understanding, relying on outside knowledge, and mismatching your points of analysis.

CHAPTER 2

COMPARING AND CONTRASTING LITERATURE: EXPERT READER MODEL

Let's see how to apply the tips and tricks to literature. Remember literature could be adventure stories, historical fiction, mysteries, myths, science fiction, realistic fiction, plays, poetry, sonnets, and more.

Developing skills to compare and contrast similar types of works, such as one myth to another myth, is important. Comparing and contrasting different genres of literature, such as a poem to a work of realistic fiction, or even a contemporary work to classic literature is equally valuable. These types of analysis can enrich your understanding of ideas, events, and themes in literary works.

Some types of literature, such as narrative fiction, often feature similar elements including characters, problems or conflicts, a setting and plot, events and episodes, and a problem resolution. Authors weave these elements together carefully, mindful that they interact in meaningful and engaging ways. Looking closely at these elements gives us a richer understanding of the story and its theme. Your comparative analysis could center on these elements.

Specific genres within literature also have specific characteristics and features. For example, science fiction contains elements of the supernatural, while realistic fiction and historical fiction include characters that are believable and events or episodes that could happen or might have happened in the past. Your analysis of two or more works of literature could center on these features, too.

Your ability to compare and contrast these components of literature relies on your grade-level knowledge of literature basics.

Charles Dickens (1812–1870) was an English writer and social critic. He created some of the world's most memorable fictional characters. Many literary experts claim that *Oliver Twist* is his most famous novel.

Plan of Action

This chapter features an excerpt from the novel *Oliver Twist* by Charles Dicken and a poem, "Chimney Sweeper," by William Blake. You'll be reading the passages and following an expert reader think through a sampling of the tips and tricks in the margin notes (refer back to the icon descriptors for guidance). It's as if you're tagging along with the expert reader.

The expert reader will then tackle some multiple-choice questions about the two passages and a constructed response question. In order to complete the constructed response question, you'll observe how the expert reader first constructs a graphic organizer that compares and contrasts critical components of both passages. All of these activities help demonstrate how to apply these crucial skills to literature.

After this, it's your turn to practice. In chapter 3, you'll be reading two passages where guided practice prompts cue your use of the tips and tricks for literature.

An Excerpt from *Oliver Twist*, Chapter 1: "The Parish Boy"
By Charles Dickens

(Note to the reader: The story of Oliver Twist *was published as a book in 1838. It tells the story of a poor orphan boy, Oliver, who survives the difficult conditions of London's underworld in the 1800s.)*

Oliver was born in the workhouse, and his mother died the same night. Not even a promised reward could produce any information as to the boy's father or the mother's name.

"How did he come to have a name at all, then?" said Mrs. Mann (who was responsible for the early bringing up of the workhouse children) to Mr. Bumble (who looked after the orphans for the parish). "I invented it," said Mr. Bumble.

At the age of nine, Oliver was removed from the tender mercies of Mrs. Mann, in whose wretched home not one kind word or look had ever

EXPERT READER:

After quickly scanning both passages, I notice that dates are included with each. In the excerpt, dates are featured in the note to the reader. In the poem, a date is featured with the title. Both dates are around the 1800s. The time period must be important. It appears the two passages share a similar historical setting.

From the note to the reader, I know that this passage takes place in London. Perhaps the two passages share London as a setting, which is an area that used chimney sweeps. I'll monitor this.

Oliver is clearly the main character, and his unique circumstance—born into a workhouse and shortly thereafter becoming an orphan—could begin to shape the problem within the story. I'll monitor this.

lighted the gloom of his infant years, and was taken into the workhouse.

There, Oliver, and his companions suffered the tortures of slow starvation. Each boy had one bowl of gruel a day. The boys grew so hungry that lots were cast who should walk up to the master after supper that evening and ask for more, and it fell to Oliver Twist. After the gruel disappeared that night, the boys nudged and winked at Oliver. Child as he was, he was desperate with hunger, and reckless with misery. He rose from the table and advancing to the master, basin and spoon in hand, said, "Please, sir, I want some more." The master was a fat, healthy man, but he turned very pale. He gazed in stupefied astonishment on the small rebel for some seconds, and then said, "What!"

The master aimed a blow at Oliver's head with the ladle and called for Mr. Bumble.

Mr. Bumble relayed news to the chairman of the board, named Limbkins. "Mr. Limbkins, I beg your pardon, sir! Oliver Twist has asked for more!" "For more?" said the chairman. "Do I understand that he asked for more, after he had eaten the supper allotted by the dietary?"

Oliver was ordered into instant confinement, and a bill was next morning posted on the outside of the workhouse gate, offering a reward of five pounds to anybody who would take Oliver Twist off their hands. In other words, five pounds and Oliver Twist were offered to any man or

This illustration depicts a scene where Oliver is led away by Mr. Bumble. The story was first published in monthly installments between 1837 and 1839 and featured black-and-white etchings, which were a type of printed illustration.

EXPERT READER:

Many adult characters are quickly introduced in this short excerpt. Here, a fee is offered to any man or woman willing to take in Oliver. All adults seem cold and ineffective. This could be a developing theme.

woman who wanted an apprentice to any trade, business, or calling.

Mr. Gamfield, the chimney sweep, was the first to respond to this offer. "It's a nasty trade," said the chairman of the board. "Young boys have been smothered in chimneys," said another member. "That's because they damped the straw afore they lit it in the chimbley to make 'em come down again," said Gamfield. "That's all smoke, and no blaze; vereas smoke only sinds him to sleep, and that ain't no use in making a boy come down. Boys is wery obstinate and wery lazy, gen'l'men, and there's nothink like a good hot blaze to make 'em come down with a run. It's a humane, too, gen'l'men, acause, even if they've stuck in the chimbley, roasting their feet make 'em struggle to hextricate theirselves."

EXPERT READER:

Although Mr. Gamfield's dialect is challenging, after rereading his comments a few times, I fear for Oliver's safety. I'm also beginning to better understand why child labor laws were enacted in the U.S. during the period of industrialization.

EXPERT READER:

As I suspected, there seems to be a lot that is shared between the passages. Charles Dickens provides a bleak glimpse into the world of chimney sweeping in *Oliver Twist*. I wonder how Blake will approach the topic in his poem.

The Chimney Sweeper
By William Blake
(This version first appeared in 1789)

When my mother died I was very young,
And my father sold me while yet my tongue
Could scarcely cry 'weep! 'weep! 'weep! 'weep!
So your chimneys I sweep, and in soot I sleep.
There's little Tom Dacre, who cried when his head,
That curled like a lamb's back, was shaved: so I said,

"Hush, Tom! never mind it, for when your head's bare,
You know that the soot cannot spoil your white hair."
And so he was quiet; and that very night,
As Tom was a-sleeping, he had such a sight—
That thousands of sweepers, Dick, Joe, Ned, and Jack,
Were all of them locked up in coffins of black.
And by came an angel who had a bright key,
And he opened the coffins and set them all free;
Then down a green plain leaping, laughing, they run,
And wash in a river, and shine in the sun.
Then naked and white, all their bags left behind,
They rise upon clouds and sport in the wind;
And the angel told Tom, if he'd be a good boy,
He'd have God for his father, and never want joy.
And so Tom awoke; and we rose in the dark,
And got with our bags and our brushes to work.
Though the morning was cold, Tom was happy and warm;
So if all do their duty they need not fear harm.

Mini Assessment

Notice that in some cases, more than one answer may be considered correct. It is important to use evidence to build a case for the best answer. Returning to the passage will be helpful.

1. What is the significance of the **note to the reader** in "The Parish Boy"?

a) It informs readers of the year in which the work was published so comparisons can be made to current practices.

EXPERT READER:

Blake has used the first person point of view to tell the tale of a child chimney sweep. The narrator shares a similar tragic background to Oliver Twist.

The interaction between the narrator and the character Tom Dacre is interesting. The narrator calms Tom by stressing the positive points of having a shaved head—the soot can't ruin it.

Unlike the Dickens passage, the children chimney sweeps are the focus in Blake's poem. The narrator shares Tom's dream about the other boys and their childlike play once freed from the "coffins" of the drudgery of their lot in life. A theme developing here seems to be the loss of youth.

The solution to the problem in this poem was that Tom took some comfort in his dream. It is also clear that he benefits from the friendship of the others, especially the narrator who instills hope in their otherwise dreary life.

b) It informs readers that the excerpt is from a well-known classic work.
c) It provides details about the main character and his misfortune as an orphan.
d) It provides details on the setting, which are critical to the theme of the passage.

2. In "The Chimney Sweeper," Tom Dacre changes from the beginning to the end of the poem. Which response _best_ describes the significance of his change?

a) Tom is comforted by the childhood images, innocence, and safety he finds in his dreams.
b) Tom begrudgingly accepts his misfortune and is thankful for his friends.
c) Tom is frightened by the kinds of harm that could come to him and is happy angles guard his safety.
d) Tom is thankful he can frolic with the other boys after they have bathed in the river.

Check your answers. Were you correct?

1. d) is the best answer. I know from my analysis that key characteristics of the setting (time and place) are critical in understanding the kinds of challenges Oliver faced. Routine practices common in London during the late 1800s are the backdrop for the events that move the plot forward.

2. a) is the correct answer. In the beginning of the poem, Tom is sad his head must be shaved whereas at the end, he is warm and happy. He believes and takes comfort in his dream.

Expert Reader: I'm satisfied with my responses. In all cases, I returned to the text to check possible answers against evidence. At times, I had to dig deeply into the text and use clues and inferences.

I'm confident I can support my answers. I'm ready to try a short constructed response question.

Question: "The Parish Boy" and "The Chimney Sweeper" both depict the life and times of orphaned children growing up in the late 1700 and early 1800s. Compare and contrast these two passages and describe how each helps build an understanding of the challenging work conditions for these children during this time period.

Expert Reader: I'll use my analysis skills to compare and contrast information from both passages. I'll begin with a plot summary and think of other elements, ideas, and themes in each. A graphic organizer will help me organize, evaluate, and prioritize my thoughts.

	"The Parish Boy"	"The Chimney Sweeper"
Plot/Summary	Oliver Twist becomes an orphan upon his mother's death (his father unknown). He lives in a workhouse until he asks for more food and is then turned out to anyone who will take him.	Narrator is a young chimney sweep who was sold by father when he was very young (his mother died). Story focuses on Tom Dacre, another young chimney sweep.
Conflicts & Challenges	Oliver is neglected, hungry, physically abused, and mistreated.	The narrator sleeps in soot, Tom cries to have his head shaved and dreams of the things he misses out on—leaping, laughing, running, and playing in the sun.
Characters (Relationship to Adults)	Mistreatment by adults—in early infancy (Mrs. Mann), in workhouse (Mr. Bumble, house master, Mr. Limbkins, and board members), and chimney sweep (Mr. Gamfield).	Absence of adult figures (yet dream contains angel and God).
Characters (Relationship to Other Children)	Referred to only as "boys" and relationship centered on obtaining more food.	The narrator is unnamed but he comforts Tom Dacre and names others, Dick, Joe, Ned, and Jack, while recounting Tom's dream.
Themes	Inept and ineffective adult nurturing, guidance, and care. Perseverance.	Loss of childhood and innocence, dreams bring some relief. Perseverance.

William Blake was an English painter and poet responsible for many works, including the poem "The Tyger" and the *Great Red Dragon* paintings.

Expert Reader: I'm pleased with my ideas and the evidence I've pulled from the passages. I'm ready to put my thoughts into writing.

Answer: Both excerpts depict the life and times of poor, orphaned children growing up around the eighteenth century. These children faced many challenges that often began with the loss of a parent, yet they did their best to devise ways to try and persevere. "The Parish Boy" provides insight into the kinds of struggles young children like Oliver faced while growing up under the care of officials in London workhouses; they were often neglected, hungry, and physically abused. Highlighted in this excerpt is the lack of effective adult guidance in helping these children improve their bleak beginnings. Mrs. Mann, Mr. Bumble, and others are inept at helping Oliver. The excerpt also suggests that working under dangerous conditions as apprentice chimney sweeps was the kind of grim future these children might expect.

"The Chimney Sweeper" accentuates the dreary reality of these unfortunate children. Specifically, we understand through Tom Dacre's dream the kind of lost childhood and innocence these children endured. The poem suggests that only through dreams could the children chimney sweeps escape the harsh reality of their daily challenges. Additionally, we learn that the children helped and supported one another as evidenced by the narrator's role in comforting Tom; unlike the earlier passage, there are no adults present in the poem. Collectively, the excerpts present us with a historical glimpse into the kind treatment poor, homeless children received and their attempts to persevere.

Conclusion

How well have you grasped the expert reader's use of the tips and tricks for comparing and contrasting texts? Decide if you're ready to move on to the guided practice in the next chapter of if you would like to take another pass through the expert reader's model.

CHAPTER 3

COMPARING AND CONTRASTING LITERATURE: GUIDED PRACTICE

Now it's time for you to apply the tips and tricks during your close reading of a passage. The practice prompt icons will guide you. Check to see if your responses to the prompts match possible responses provided in the chapter.

This sixteenth-century oil painting depicts a scene from *Icarus and Daedalus,* a story featured in the guided practice that follows.

Icarus and Daedalus

Daedalus once built for King Minos of Crete, a wonderful Labyrinth so cunningly tangled up that, once inside, you could never find your way out again without a magic clue. But the king's favor veered, and one day he had his master architect imprisoned in a tower. Daedalus managed to escape from his cell; but it seemed impossible to leave the island, since every ship that came or went was well guarded by order of the king.

Watching the sea-gulls in the air, he thought of a plan for himself and his young son Icarus, who was captive with him. Little by little, he gathered a store of feathers great and small. He fastened these together with thread, molded them in with wax, and so fashioned two great wings like those of a bird. When they were done, Daedalus fitted them to his own shoulders, and after one or two efforts, he found that by waving his arms he could fly.

Without delay, he began work on a pair of wings for the boy Icarus, and taught him carefully how to use them, bidding him beware of rash adventures among the stars. "Remember," said the father, "never to fly very low or very high, for the fogs about the earth would weigh you down, but the blaze of the sun will surely melt your feathers apart if you go too near."

GUIDED PRACTICE PROMPT:

What jump-start clues do you notice? Possible response: I notice that the title of each passage is likely the name of the main characters. This follows the structure of many myths. I suspect that I might be comparing two Greek myths.

How can you use text structure to help find the theme? Possible response: Details confirm that this is a Greek myth. I know myths were used to teach and explain events. The structure of the text also suggests that a problem in the story is that Daedalus is imprisoned on an island.

GUIDED PRACTICE PROMPT:

How can a breakdown of literary elements help here? Possible response: Icarus, a new character, is introduced to the story. I'll monitor the significance of his role.

GUIDED PRACTICE PROMPT:

What are you thinking? Possible response: I'm thinking that something might happen as a result of Icarus's disregard of his father's advice. Perhaps I misidentified the larger problem in this myth.

For Icarus, these cautions went in at one ear and out by the other. Who could remember to be careful when he was to fly for the first time? Are birds careful? Not they! And not an idea remained in the boy's head but the one joy of escape.

The day came, and the father bird put on his wings, and he waited to see that all was well with Icarus. Up they rose, the boy after his father. The hateful ground of Crete sank beneath them. At first there was a terror in the joy. The wide vacancy of the air dazed them,—a glance downward made their brains reel. But when a great wind filled their wings, and Icarus felt himself sustained, like a bird, like a child uplifted by his mother, he forgot everything in the world but joy. He longed for one draught of flight to quench the thirst of his captivity: he stretched out his arms to the sky and made towards the highest heavens.

GUIDED PRACTICE PROMPT:

Are you being attentive to the author? Possible response: In his joy of freedom, Icarus has forgotten his father's warning. The comparisons made to a bird's flight and to the uplifting of a mother explain how Icarus's emotional reaction outweighed his caution.

What are you thinking? Possible response: Now I understand that this myths was probably used to teach children obedience. It also warns that getting lost in emotion can be tragic.

Alas for him! Warmer and warmer grew the air. His wings wavered, drooped. He fluttered his young hands vainly,—he was falling,—and in that terror he remembered. The heat of the sun had melted the wax from his wings; the feathers were falling, one by one, like snowflakes; and there was none to help.

He fell like a leaf tossed down the wind, down, down. When Daedalus returned, and sought high and low for the poor boy, he saw nothing but the bird-like feathers afloat on the water, and he knew that Icarus was drowned.

Phaethon
from *Old Greek Folk Stories Told Anew*
by Josephine Preson

GUIDED PRACTICE PROMPT:

What are you thinking? Possible response: Already I'm guessing a common feature these two myths may share is a father/son relationship.

There were two playmates, said to be of heavenly parentage. One was Epaphus, who claimed Zeus as a father; and one was Phaethon, the earthly child of Apollo. One day they were boasting, each of his own father, and Epaphus, angry at the other's fine story, dared him to prove his kinship with the Sun.

Phaethon went to his mother, Clymene. "It is true, my child," she said, "If you have any doubt, go to the land whence the sun rises at morning and ask of him

This illustration depicts a scene from *Phaethon*. The vivid images show the kind of severe lessons that are often found in Greek mythology.

🖥 GUIDED PRACTICE PROMPT:

How can you use text structure here? Possible response: This type of conflict—an inability to refuse a request—could foreshadow the problem. I'll monitor this yet may change my thinking based on text evidence as I did in the first myth.

any gift you will; he is your father, and he cannot refuse you."

Phaethon journeyed till he came to the palace of the Sun. He entered and beheld a glorious being, none other than Apollo himself, seated upon a throne. Round his head there shone a blinding light. "O my father," stammered Phaethon, "if you are my father indeed," and then he took courage; for the god came down from his throne, put off the glorious halo that hurt mortal eyes, and embraced him tenderly.

"Indeed, thou art my son," said he. "Ask any gift of me and it shall be thine"; "Ah!" cried Phaethon rapturously. "Let me drive thy chariot for one day!" For an instant the Sun's looks clouded. "Choose again, my child," said he. "Thou art only a mortal, and this task is mine alone of all the gods. Not Zeus himself dare drive the chariot of the Sun. The way is full of terrors, both for the horses and for all the stars, and for the Earth. Listen, and choose again." But these counsels only made the reckless boy more eager. "I will take care," he begged. Apollo was forced to keep his promise.

🖥 GUIDED PRACTICE PROMPT:

How can a breakdown of literary elements help here? Possible response: In this myth, the characters and setting involve mortals and gods, and Earth and heavens.

What are you thinking? Possible response: The warning Apollo gives Phaethon sounds almost identical to the warnings Daedalus gives Icarus.

Already the stars were beginning to wane. The courtiers harnessed the four horses. Wild, immortal steeds they were, untamed as the winds. "Follow the road," said Apollo, "Go not too high or too low, for the sake of heavens and earth; else men and gods will suffer."

Phaethon took his place in the chariot, gathered up the reins, and the horses sprang away. As they went, they bent their splendid necks to see the meaning of the strange hand upon the reins and neighed one to another. It was holiday for the horses of the Sun, and away they went. Grasping the reins that dragged him after, like an enemy, Phaethon looked down from the fearful ascent and saw the Earth far beneath him. He was blind and dizzy with bewilderment. His hold slackened and the horses redoubled their speed. They left the old tracks. Before he knew where he was, they had startled the constellations and grazed the Serpent, so that it woke and hissed.

The steeds took fright. This way and that they went, terrified by the monsters they had never encountered before. Up, far above the clouds, they went, and down again, towards the defenseless Earth, that could not flee from the chariot of the Sun. Great rivers hid themselves in the ground, mountains were consumed, and harvests perished like a moth singed in a candle-flame.

GUIDED PRACTICE PROMPT:

How can you use text structure here? Possible response: The problem in this story spirals. Apollo was unable to refuse his son's request, Phaethon loses control of the horses, and they awaken the serpent.

Are you being attentive to the author? Possible response: Unlike the earlier myth, the consequences in this one are more severe; Phaethon jeopardizes Earth and all mortals living upon it. The personification of Earth arouses our feelings for her even beyond our feelings for Phaethon.

In vain did Phaethon call to the horses and pull upon the reins. He saw his own Earth, his beautiful home and the home of all men, parched by the fires of this mad chariot. The poor Earth lifted her withered face in a last prayer to Zeus to save them if he might. Then Zeus, calling all the gods to witness that there was no other means of safety, hurled his thunderbolt; and Phaethon knew no more. His body fell through the heavens, aflame like a shooting-star; and the horses of the Sun dashed homeward with the empty chariot.

GUIDED PRACTICE PROMPT:

How can you use text structure here? Possible response: In both myths, each main character loses his life as a part of the solution to the problem.

Mini Assessment

Notice that in some cases, more than one answer may be considered correct. It is important to use evidence to build a case for the best answer. Returning to the passage will be helpful.

1. Which sentence from *Icarus and Daedalus* best supports the main problem in the myth?

    a) But the king's favor veered with the wind, and one day he had his master architect imprisoned in a tower.

    b) For Icarus, these cautions went in at one ear and out by the other.

    c) At first, there was terror in the joy.

    d) The day came, and the father bird put on his wings, and he waited to see that all was well with Icarus.

2. Reread the following sentence from *Phaethon*: "Thou art only a mortal, and this task is mine alone of all the gods." What purpose does this sentence serve?

    a) It explains why the horses neighed one to another and felt they could take a holiday.

    b) It explains why Zeus hurled his thunderbolt.

    c) It explains why Apollo asks Phaethon to select another gift.

    d) It explains why the defenseless Earth prayed to Zeus.

Check your answers. Were you correct?

    1. b) is the best answer. The cautions his father gave him were ignored, which caused Icarus's unfortunate death.

    2. c) is the best answer. Apollo recognizes the magnitude of his task and tries to impart this wisdom to Phaethon.

What do you think so far? Is your understanding and analysis of the passages taking shape? Did you return to the passages and find evidence to support your responses? Are you comfortable using a graphic organizer to collect evidence to answer a short constructed response question and then discussing or writing a response? Again, either talk through your answer or jot it down on a separate piece of paper. (See the expert reader's response for guidance).

Question: In both myths, characters exhibit a form of recklessness, which leads to much misery and loss. How are these myths the same and how are they different? In your response, compare and contrast the two variations using details from both myths to support your answer.

Possible Graphic Organizer and Response

	Icarus and Daedalus	*Phaethon*
Plot/Summary	Icarus and Daedalus are imprisoned on an island yet escape using wings made of wax and feathers. Icarus flies too close to the sun, his wings melt, and he drowns.	Phaethon pleas with Apollo to drive the sun chariot. He loses control of the horses, scorches Earth, and is sent out of the sky by Zeus's thunderbolt.
Conflicts & Challenges	Icarus does not heed his father's warnings. He is reckless and becomes lost in the joy of escape.	Phaethon does not heed his father's advice. He is boastful and seeks recognition.
Characters	Icarus and Daedalus are mortals.	Phaethon is a mortal. Apollo, the horses, and Zeus are immortals.
Themes	Obedience, humility, recklessness	Obedience, humility, recklessness, the importance of honoring and respecting the Gods

Possible Response

Recklessness is a common theme found within the two Greek myths *Icarus and Daedalus* and *Phaethon*. Both myths warn that tragic outcomes may result when recklessness replaces good judgment—especially the kind of good judgment that stems from a parent's wisdom. Icarus ignores his father's advice and flies too close to the sun. Although it's easy to grasp how the joy and adventure of soaring to freedom may have been distracting, Icarus still paid dearly with his life.

Phaethon was also reckless, yet unlike Icarus, his stemmed from boastfulness and a lack of humility. As the immortal son of Apollo, Phaethon tragically misjudged the magnitude of driving the immortal steeds and chariot, a task meant solely for Apollo. Like Icarus, Phaethon was warned by his father, who pleaded that he chose another gift. Like Icarus, his recklessness was unforgiveable and nearly resulted in the destruction of all things on and including Earth. In addition to teaching a very valuable life lesson about the importance of obedience, both myths also serve as a reverent reminder of the greatness of the Greek gods; mortals like Icarus, Daedalus, and Phaethon have no place in the heavens, which is home only to the gods.

Conclusion

How well have you grasped the tips and tricks for comparing and contrasting literature? Based on your performance and self-evaluation, decide if you're ready to move on to the next chapter or if you would like to take another pass through this guided practice.

CHAPTER 4

COMPARING AND CONTRASTING INFORMATIONAL TEXTS: EXPERT READER MODEL

Now, let's see how to apply the tips and tricks to informational text. Informational text is a type of nonfiction, or factual text, that is written to inform the reader, explain something, or convey information about the natural and social worlds. Informational text can include newspaper or magazine articles, essays, speeches, opinion pieces, editorials, and historical, scientific, or technical accounts. Developing skills to compare and contrast one author's presentation of events with that of another is important. Analyzing how two or more authors shape their presentations of key information by emphasizing different evidence or by advancing different interpretations of facts is equally important, as is being able to analyze two or more texts that provide conflicting information on the same topic.

Authors of informational text have a point to make about a topic. They frequently want to change your thinking in some way or add to your understanding. Looking closely at how two or more authors shape their presentations can help you detect and explore similarities and differences and distinguish between critical and noncritical points of analysis. Awareness of these types of strategies helps a reader compare and contrast text and improves comprehension.

Plan of Action

The passages in this chapter are excerpts from *Tattoos and Indigenous People* and *Tattooing: Why People Get Tattoos and Other Body Art*. Similar to chapter 2, you'll be reading the excerpts while following an expert reader think through the tips and tricks; this time as they are applied to informational text. You may want to refresh your memory by reviewing the tips and tricks on pages 9–12 before beginning.

Again, you'll observe the expert reader work through some multiple-choice questions, followed by the sharing of a graphic organizer and a constructed response, to get the full impact of how to compare and contrast informational text.

Then, in the chapter that follows, it will be your turn to practice. You'll start by reading a passage where guided practice prompts and icons cue your use of the tips and tricks. You can check your thinking against possible responses that are located later in the chapter.

EXPERT READER:

I notice there are two separate passages here. Both have "tattoo" in the title. I'm uncertain what "indigenous" means, so I'll look for a definition as I read. A quick glance at headings will give me some insight before I read.

I know I can use headings and paragraph structure to help me determine central ideas. Central ideas emerge early and develop throughout the passage. I'll use the headings to guide me as I read through each section to determine what information the author stresses.

An Excerpt from
Tattoos and Indigenous People
 by Judith Levin

Introduction

When "tribal" tattoos began to be fashionable in the 1980s, people admired them for their bold black patterns. Many tribal tattoos are based on designs from islands in the Pacific Ocean. But if you go back in time, you

Tattoos were a part of many indigenous cultures and were viewed as an important form of communication.

would find many more styles of tribal tattoos worn by indigenous peoples. Indigenous peoples are the cultural groups and their descendants who lived in a region before it was discovered and taken over by another people. Many indigenous peoples were tribal and lived in extended family groups. Anthropologists have discovered that indigenous cultures spent a long time—sometimes thousands of years—creating stories and rituals and art. In many places, these arts included tattooing.

> ### 📖 EXPERT READER:
>
> I know what "indigenous" means now. I'm now thinking I'll be reading about how tattoos are reflective of a particular group of people's way of life.

What Indigenous Tattoos Mean

Tattoos were a way of communicating. They said to other people in the same group, "I am old enough to get married" or "I am brave enough to be a hunter." They said to others in the region, "Hands off! This person belongs to us." They said to gods or helpful spirits, "I ask for your help and your protection" or "This tattoo marks the part of my body that hurts. Could you make it stop hurting?" They said "By getting this tattoo, I show that I am one of Us"—part of a particular family or tribe.

> ### 📖 EXPERT READER:
>
> This paragraph seems important—the first sentence seems critical. Tattoos weren't merely for decoration. They were a form of communication for indigenous people.

In 1991, the 5,000 year old frozen body of a man was discovered in the mountains near Italy. On the inside of his left knee was tattooed a black cross, six straight lines were on his lower back, and many parallel lines were tattooed on his ankles, legs, and wrists. When x-rayed, evidence of joint disease was found under each tattoo. The Egyptian god Bes was found tattooed on female mummies. Bes was the god of women in labor and would protect them during this dangerous time. In 1993, the tattooed body of a woman was found in Siberia. Her tattoos were among the most detailed and beautiful found from this early period. She was buried with beautiful and expensive objects, which shows that tattoos were worn by people of high status. ⊤

> **⛉ EXPERT READER:**
>
> ⊤ The examples in this paragraph support how tattoos communicated information. I've never connected tattoos and communication before, but I can see the connection now.

Marks of Shame

For Greeks and Romans, tattoos were marks of shame, not honor. They felt tattoos showed that tribal people were barbarians and tattooed the foreheads of slaves who tried to escape. One emperor punished two monks by tattooing obscene poetry on their foreheads. In Japan, tattoos were used as punishment and a criminal would have the word meaning "bad" or "evil" tattooed on his forehead. People who had been tattooed for committing a crime could never be part of society again. Their punishment was forever, so some began to make decorations of them, hiding their shameful tattoos under beautiful ones, such as pictures of mountains.))

> **⛉ EXPERT READER:**
>
>)) The author provides more support for the idea that tattoos were used to communicate many types of messages. I'm seeing the central idea emerge.

Samoan Tattoos

On the Polynesian island of Somoa, a boy who did not get tattooed at puberty could not become a man. He would be a man biologically, in his body, but he would not be a man *culturally*. He could not marry, had to remain silent when the men were speaking, and could never become chief. Samoan women were tattooed with designs resembling lace or

📖 EXPERT READER:

 Details in this paragraph further support communication as a central idea. I'm understanding that tattoos were an important part of indigenous peoples' lives because they provided communication to people within groups, as well as outside the group.

flowers on their face, arms, and hands. A woman without tattoos on her hands was denied the honor of serving *kava*, a special ceremonial drink. Both men and women showed their commitment to their culture by getting tattoos. 📖

📖 EXPERT READER:

I know why indigenous people got tattoos. What can I add to my understanding as I read this excerpt?

An Excerpt from
Tattooing: Why People Get Tattoos and Other Body Art
by Jeanne Nagle

Introduction

People seem to like tinkering with their image. A new hairstyle or color, or applying makeup in a unique way are examples of fairly simple changes that can be made to one's looks. There are some modifications that are more permanent, however, such as piercing, tattooing, and earlobe stretching. The decision to permanently alter one's body is a serious one. A person should never get a tattoo as a way to fit in or try out a passing style or trend. The first step in making a wise decision about whether or not to get a tattoo is to be well informed about the benefits and risks.

📖 EXPERT READER:

 In the first excerpt, the author stressed tattoos as a way of communicating belonging to a group. This author warns not to get a tattoo to fit in. I think I'm going to get another viewpoint in this excerpt with a group. I'll be alert to stressed information that leads to the central idea of this excerpt.

Self-Expression and Self-Image

There are numerous ways people can express their individuality. Because

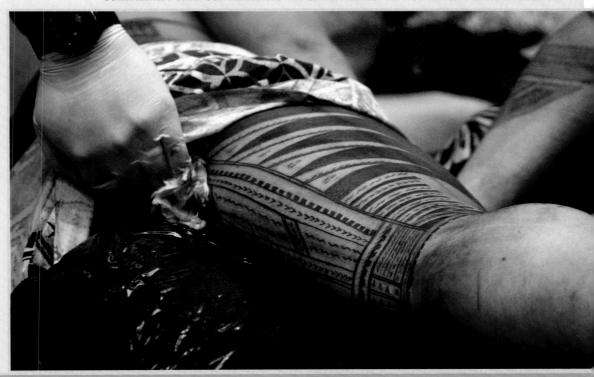

The decision to get a tattoo is a serious one that deserves careful consideration.

tattoos help change their appearance, many people, particularly those in their teens and twenties, believe tattoos are an excellent form of self-expression. Getting a tattoo is a personal matter. Many others may choose the same tattoo image, but it will look different on, and mean different things to, each wearer.

There are times in people's lives when they may discover a new passion in their life or they take part in an activity that makes them happy and has a positive

📖 EXPERT READER:

Tattoos as a way to communicate individuality and self-expression is discussed here while identification with a group was stressed in the first article.

influence on them. A tattoo is a lasting reminder of how they felt at that time. Some people tattoo landmarks as a visual reminder of a favorite trip. Others get a tattoo to remain close to someone or something they've lost. Some people use tattoos to remember major events that might have made them feel like a new person, such as turning twenty-one, getting married, having a baby, or surviving a medical crisis. Some people choose to have medical alerts tattooed on their skin to let health care providers know about a medical condition in the event they are unable to communicate.

Getting a tattoo is usually a sign that someone takes pride in their appearance, but there is another type of pride associated with tattooing, and that is pride in one's identity. Elements of a person's identity that he or she might want to boast about through a tattoo include nationality, family heritage, career, and personal accomplishments. Tattoos can also serve as a symbol of inspiration, giving the wearer the courage to take action and go forward with a plan. At other times, a tattoo will not convey any special meaning and may just be meant to be colorful and attractive. ⟋

🕮 EXPERT READER:

⟋ The author gives many examples of how tattoos can be used to express individuality. Although important to the individual, a person's tattoo could really mean nothing to others in his/her cultural group. This is a different idea than was discussed in the first excerpt.

Think Before You Ink

Tattoos send a message to people you meet. People may attach different meanings to those messages—some of them negative. While some people might see tattoos as fashionable, hip, and adventurous, others will interpret ink as a statement against mainstream society. Others tend to think tattoos may be an indication that the wearer engages in risky behaviors. Put simply, having a tattoo might get a person "in" with some crowds, but keep them on the fringes of others. Anybody who is thinking about getting a tattoo should seriously consider the social implications beforehand. 📖

📖 **EXPERT READER:**

Each section and paragraph in this excerpt stresses how tattoos are used to communicate individuality. I think the central idea in this excerpt is tattoos are currently used to communicate individuality. This central idea is similar, yet different from the first excerpt in a significant way.

Mini Assessment

Notice that in some cases, more than one answer may be considered correct. It is important to use evidence to build a case for the *best* answer. Carefully reviewing evidence by returning to the passage will be helpful.

1. Which sentence from *Tattoos and Indigenous People* <u>best</u> supports the central idea of this passage?

a) Many tribal tattoos are based on designs from islands in the Pacific Ocean.

b) They said to other people in the same group, "I am old enough to be married" or "I am brave enough to be a hunter."

c) Her tattoos were among the most detailed and beautiful found from this early period.

d) Their punishments were forever, so some began to make decorations of them, hiding their shameful tattoos under beautiful ones, such as pictures of mountains.

2. In the section "Think Before You Ink" from *Tattooing: Why People Get Tattoos and Other Body Art*, how does the author establish the idea that tattoos are a powerful form of communication?

a) By revealing that some people see tattoos as fashionable.

b) By explaining that tattoos send a message to people you meet.

c) By arguing that having a tattoo might get a person "in" with some crowds, but keep them on the fringes of others.

d) By suggesting that a person should be well informed before getting a tattoo.

Check your answers. Were you correct?

1. b) is the best answer. I know from my analysis of the excerpt that the central idea of this passage is that tattoos were used as a form of communication. Tattoos "spoke" to people in groups and told something about the person wearing the tattoo.

2. c) is the best answer. The purpose of the section "Think Before You Ink" was to stress how tattoos may send messages that the wearer hadn't thought of and that the communication the tattoo sends may make the wearer accepted in some groups, but may also keep the wearer out of other groups he or she may want to be in.

Expert Reader: I'm satisfied with my responses. In all cases, I returned to the text to check possible answers against evidence. At times, I had to dig deeply into the text and use clues and inferences while carefully weighing my thinking. I'm confident I can argue in support of my answers with credible evidence from the text. I'm ready to try a short constructed response question.

Question: *Tattoos and Indigenous People* and *Tattooing: Why People Get Tattoos and Other Body Art*, both discuss the purposes and effects of tattoos. How have the purposes and effects of tattoos changed throughout history? How have the purposes and effects of tattoos remained the same? Use details from both articles to support your answer.

Expert Reader: I'll need to use my analysis skills to compare and contrast information from both of the excerpts I've read about tattoos to answer this question. A graphic organizer will help me weigh the evidence and select the most important details from the excerpts to use in my constructed response.

	Purpose of Tattoo	Effect of Tattoo
Tattoos and Indigenous People	-Way to communicate with people in own group, people outside group, and gods or spirits	-People in same group knew person belonged -People in outside groups knew which group person belonged to -Gods and spirits knew where to heal body or protect person from harm
	-To show commitment to culture	-Somoan boys are tattooed to show that they are men culturally -Somoan women are tattooed so that they can have the honor of serving a special ceremonial drink
Tattooing: Why People Get Tattoos and Other Body Art	-To express individuality	-Tattoo means something to wearer, but others may not know meaning -May get wearer "in" with some groups -May keep wearer "out" of other groups -Possible negative social implications
	-To act as a lasting reminder	-Visual reminder of favorite trip, someone lost, major life event

Expert Reader: I'm satisfied with the evidence I've collected to answer the short response question and am now ready to put my thoughts into writing.

Answer: It is evident from both excerpts that the purpose of tattoos is communication. What tattoos communicate and the effect of that communication have changed throughout history, however. For example, many times indigenous peoples used tattoos as a way to communicate belonging and their association with a certain group of people. Tattoos would identify them as a member of the group and offer them protection when they traveled away from the group. They also used tattoos as a way to communicate with gods and spirits to ask for their healing or protection for tattooed body areas. On the island of Somoa, boys communicated their commitment to their culture by receiving tattoos at puberty. By receiving a tattoo, the men showed that they belonged to the group and would abide by their cultural customs. Likewise, women who did not have tattooed hands could not serve special ceremonial drinks. These tattoos bound them to their cultural group.

People in modern times still use tattoos as a way to communicate, but many times these tattoos express the wearer's individuality as opposed to belonging to a larger group. While the tattoo may be meaningful to the wearer, others viewing the tattoo may not be aware of that meaning. For instance, a tattoo may memorialize something from an individual's life that is of little significance to others from his or her cultural group. When there is no understanding of the meaning for the tattoo, it can sometimes be viewed as a statement against mainstream society and work to keep the wearer on the fringes of social groups. This is quite different than the indigenous tattoos that bound people together.

How well do you feel you've grasped the expert reader's use of the tips and tricks for comparing and contrasting texts? Decide if you're ready to move on to the guided practice in the next chapter or if you would like to take another pass through the expert reader's model.

CHAPTER 5

COMPARING AND CONTRASTING INFORMATIONAL TEXTS: GUIDED PRACTICE

Next, it's time for you to apply the tips and tricks during your close reading of a passage. The practice prompt icons will guide you. Check to see if your responses to the prompts match possible responses provided in the chapter.

🏃 An Excerpt from *America Debates Global Warming: Crisis or Myth?*
by Matthew Robinson

Global Warming

Global warming isn't much more complicated than it sounds. It is simply the slow warming of our planet's atmosphere and surface over time. Usually when you hear the phrase "global warming" on the news or at school, you can bet

🖥 GUIDED PRACTICE PROMPT:

🏃 What jump-start clues do you notice? Possible response: After a quick scan, I notice that global warming is the common topic of these two excerpts and that the word "debate" is in each title. I know debates are discussions where two opposing arguments are put forward, so I'm guessing I'll be comparing and contrasting arguments that have to do with global warming.

they are talking about global warming caused by human beings. Global warming takes place naturally, too, but many scientists believe the type of global warming occurring today is very different from warming caused by nature.

Climate Change

Climate change, like global warming, again isn't much more complicated than it sounds. It simply means a slow change in Earth's climate. If the climate is changing, then it would be nothing new for our planet. Earth has

Global warming is the slow warming of the planet's atmosphere and surface over time, and it can occur naturally or be caused by humans.

been subjected to severe climate changes in the past. The many ice ages the planet has gone through were all severe climate changes. And yet, the type of climate change being experienced today has a lot of people very worried. They believe there is a lot of reliable, scientific data that says the present climate change is different from any that has taken place before.

Is Global Warming Happening Now?

Just about every respectable scientist agrees that, yes, over the past twenty years, global temperatures have been rising. What some disagree on is whether this warming trend will continue, whether it is caused by human activity, and if it is anything to be worried about. Global temperatures have been documented since 1860. Out of the twenty-one hottest years since 1860, twenty have taken place in just the past twenty-five years. ↗

> **GUIDED PRACTICE PROMPT:**
>
> ↗ How can a breakdown of literary elements help here? Possible response: The author is giving me a lot of background knowledge on global warming so that I can begin to make connections among and distinctions between the two sides of the debate. Scientists agree temperatures are rising, but why?

Reading Ice Cores

Recently, scientists discovered a new way of using ice samples to read the planet's temperatures far earlier than just 1860. They drill very deep into ice that froze a long time ago to find air bubbles that were frozen in the snow and ice from up to 700,000 years ago. The bubbles tell them what the temperature was back then. The results of testing show a world where temperatures have risen in the past 30 years like they've never risen before.

> **GUIDED PRACTICE PROMPT:**
>
> What are you thinking? Possible response: Here is more information to support the claim that world temperatures are rising, but why?

Sea Levels

Another way to find out if global temperatures are rising is to look at sea levels, which are the average water levels in the oceans around the world. When scientists observe high tide coming up higher and higher, then they know the sea levels are rising. Higher sea levels are related to rising global temperatures in two ways. First, warm water expands so if global temperatures are rising, then the oceans will expand and the sea levels rise. The melting of sea ice and glaciers is another reason why global warming is related to sea levels. When ice melts, it no longer floats on top of the ocean and instead flows into the ocean, thus causing the sea levels to rise.

 GUIDED PRACTICE PROMPT:

 Are you being attentive to the way the author is presenting information? Possible response: This author clearly explains the evidence that supports the fact that global warming is happening.

Can Human Beings Cause Global Warming?

The majority of scientists in the world today believe there is a connection between global warming and humans' burning of fossil fuels. Fossil fuels are what we use to power most of the technology that runs our world. Gasoline, coal, oil, and natural gases are all fossil fuels. These energy sources are used to produce electricity and give us light, heat, and the ability to run electronic devices. Almost all modern technology relies on fossil fuels. When fossil fuels are burned to extract their energy, they release carbon dioxide. When there is too much carbon dioxide in the atmosphere, less heat escapes into space and our Earth begins to warm up.

GUIDED PRACTICE PROMPT:

What are you thinking? Possible response: Now I understand the connection between global warming and humans. Our reliance on fossil fuels to provide energy to run all our technology is causing a big problem. Too much carbon dioxide in the atmosphere equals global warming. Humans seem to have control over whether global warming continues or not.

An Excerpt from
Debating the Issue: Global Warming
by L.H. Colligan

What Is Global Warming?
Global warming is not the local weather forecast, a summer heat wave, or a few warm winters. It is the rise in the average land and ocean temperatures on planet Earth. Since the mid-1800s, the worldwide average temperature has been going up with warm extremes coming twice as often as the cold extremes.

Running Hot and Cold
Throughout its four-and-a-half-billion-year history, natural events called climate forcings have sometimes made Earth colder and sometimes warmer than it is now. Natural forcings include the sun, Earth's orbit around the sun, ocean currents, volcanoes, clouds, and gases.

Some climatologists and environmentalists who measure Earth's health say the biggest, most damaging climate forcing ever is taking place now. This forcing, they say, is not the sun, ocean currents, earthquakes, or volcanoes—it is the human race. Other scientists contend that humans are not powerful enough to change something as big as the climate. The two sides are arguing about greenhouse gases, the heat-trapping substances that protect the planet from the sun and cold.

GUIDED PRACTICE PROMPT:

What are you thinking? Possible response: I know there is a debate over global warming. The first excerpt gave me a lot of background knowledge and explained one cause for global warming: humans. Maybe I'll get the opposing argument in this excerpt.

What are you thinking? Possible response: This information is consistent with that in the first excerpt—Earth is getting warmer.

GUIDED PRACTICE PROMPT:

How can a breakdown of literary elements help here? Possible response: Here's some new information to consider—Natural events called climate forcings cause global warming and humans are not powerful enough to change climate. I don't usually hear this side of the debate, so I'll continue reading carefully to build my understanding and knowledge.

Is It Getting Hotter or Not?

Climate experts on different sides of the global warming debate pretty much agree on one thing: the Earth has gotten warmer for at least a hundred years. The debate comes down to this: are human activities that increase carbon dioxide levels, like fossil fuel burning, causing global warming? Many scientists say no and suggest that we "look to nature" for an explanation.

Climatologists call the period between around 1300 and 1850 the Little Ice Age. During most of those centuries, the average temperature drop is thought to have been 1.8 degrees Fahrenheit. While this may seem small, the negative effects lasted for centuries. Professor of meteorology Reid Bryson says "Of course (the temperature) is going up. It has gone up since the early 1800s, before the Industrial Revolution, because we're coming out of the Little Ice Age, not because we're putting more carbon dioxide into the air."

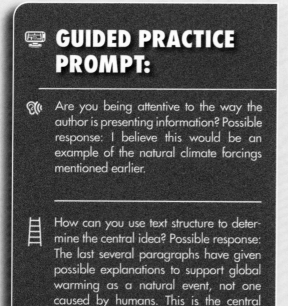

GUIDED PRACTICE PROMPT:

Are you being attentive to the way the author is presenting information? Possible response: I believe this would be an example of the natural climate forcings mentioned earlier.

How can you use text structure to determine the central idea? Possible response: The last several paragraphs have given possible explanations to support global warming as a natural event, not one caused by humans. This is the central idea of this excerpt.

The Oceans

Oceans and their currents are such powerful forcings, some oceanographers say, that they change climate much more than humans ever could. William M. Gray, a professor of atmospheric science, argues that "This small warming is likely a result of the natural alterations in the global ocean currents, which are driven by ocean salinity (salt level) variations ....Humankind has little or nothing to do with the recent temperature changes. We are not that influential."

Skeptical Experts Look at the Future

How do those who reject human-caused global warming see the future? Some point out something that ought to be obvious: people have built successful societies in places with huge temperature difference. They argue that humans are an adaptable species. New technologies can help humans adjust to climate change that may come. For example, a hundred years ago, Florida, Texas, and Arizona were lightly populated and

Is the burning of fossil fuels causing global warming? Scientists can provide evidence to support both sides of the debate that come with answering this question.

💻 GUIDED PRACTICE PROMPT:

🗨 What are you thinking? No one really knows for certain why global warming is happening. People who support this side of the debate believe there's nothing humans can do to stop or slow down global warming so that we better find ways to adapt to the warmer temperatures. Would these new technologies rely on the burning of fossil fuels to provide energy to power them? This is something to think about.

considered almost unliveable for a good part of the year. Thanks to the invention of air-conditioning, the population of those states has boomed. 🗨

Mini Assessment

Again, be aware that it is important to use evidence to build a case for the *best* answer. Remember to carefully review evidence by returning to the passage to gauge which response is best supported.

1. Which sentence from *America Debates Global Warming: Crisis or Myth?* best supports the <u>central idea</u> of this passage?

    a) They believe there is a lot of reliable, scientific data that says that present climate change is different from any that has taken place before.

    b) Out of the twenty-one hottest years since 1860, twenty have taken place in just the past twenty-five years.

    c) When fossil fuels are burned to extract their energy, they release carbon dioxide.

    d) The melting of sea ice and glaciers is another reason why global warming is related to sea levels.

2. Which sentence from *Debating the Issue: Global Warming* most clearly supports the position that humans are not powerful enough to change something as big as climate?

    a) The forcing, they say, is not the sun, ocean, currents, earthquakes, or volcanoes—it is the human race.

    b) It (the temperature) has gone up since the early 1800s, before the Industrial Revolution, because we're coming out of the

Little Ice Age, not because we are putting more carbon dioxide into the air.

c) Climate experts on different sides of the global warming debate pretty much agree on one thing: Earth has gotten warmer for at least a hundred years.

d) New technologies can help humans adjust to climate change that may come.

Check your answers. Were you correct?

1. c) is the best answer. The central idea of this excerpt is that humans are causing global warming through the burning of fossil fuels to power our technology. c) best supports this idea.

2. b) is the best answer. The central idea of this excerpt is that global warming is a natural event and not one that is caused by humans. Humans are not powerful enough to affect natural events, like ice ages. We have no control over them.

What do you think so far? Is your understanding and analysis of the passages taking shape? Did you return to the passages and find evidence to support your responses? Did your answers square with the evidence? Are you comfortable using a graphic organizer to collect evidence to answer a short constructed response question and then discussing or writing a response? Again, either talk through your answer or jot it down on a separate piece of paper. (See the expert reader's response for guidance.)

Question: Compare and contrast both sides of the global warming debate addressed in the excerpts from *America Debates Global Warming: Crisis or Myth?* and *Debating the Issue: Global Warming.* Discuss how the interpretation of data affects the solutions that have been suggested to address global warming.

Possible Graphic Organizer and Response

	Cause of Global Warming	Solution to Global Warming
America Debates Global Warming: Crisis or Myth?	Human Beings -Reliance on fossil fuels like gasoline, coal, oil, natural gases -Fossil fuels power most of modern technology that runs our world -When burned to produce energy, fossil fuels release carbon dioxide -Too much carbon dioxide in atmosphere, less heat escapes into space and Earth warms	-Stop burning fossil fuels -Find alternate energy sources
Debating the Issue: Global Warming	Nature -Climate forcings -Earth coming out of Little Ice Age (1300–1850) -Natural alterations in global ocean currents. Currents affect temperatures	-Develop new technologies to help humans adapt to warmer temperatures

Possible Response

Both sides of the global warming debate agree that temperatures on Earth are increasing. The debate begins when the causes for global warming are explored. One side of the debate believes that human beings are directly responsible for global warming, while the other side believes that human beings have little to do with the warming and that nature is the cause. Both sides of the debate view global warming as a problem, but solutions are quite different depending on the position one takes as to the causes.

One side of the debate believes that human beings' reliance on fossil fuels like gasoline, coal, oil, and natural gas is the cause of global warming. Fossil fuels power most of the modern technology that runs our world today. When burned to produce energy, fossil fuels release carbon dioxide. When there is too much carbon dioxide in the atmosphere, less heat escapes into space and Earth warms. When global warming is viewed in this manner, the solution is obvious: stop burning fossil fuels and find alternate energy sources.

The other side of the debate believes that human beings have nothing to do with global warming and that nature and natural climate forcing is the cause. This view is supported by the data that reveals that Earth is coming out of a period of time called the Little Ice Age, so of course, the temperature is increasing. Natural alterations in global ocean currents that affect global temperatures are also a cause that cannot be controlled by humans. Supporters of this position feel that humans need to begin developing new technologies that will help them adapt to the warmer temperatures since they can't do anything to stop it because it is being caused by nature. It is interesting to note that on one side of the debate, technology is the source of the problem, while on the other side, technology is viewed as the solution to the problem.

Conclusion

How well have you grasped the tips and tricks for comparing and contrasting informational text? Based on your performance and self-evaluations, decide if you've mastered the skills or if you would like to take another pass through this guided practice. Congratulations if you're ready to move on.

A New Expert Reader!

Now that you've mastered how to use the tips and tricks for comparing and contrasting texts, you're on your way to becoming an expert reader! Continue to practice with different types of literature and informational text. You'll see that your attempts to grapple with classroom and assigned texts are far easier now.

GLOSSARY

ANALYZE To carefully examine, inspect, and consider a text in order to fully understand it.

CENTRAL IDEA The key concept or message being expressed.

CLOSE READING The deep, analytical reading of a brief passage of text in which the reader constructs meaning based on author intention and text evidence. The close reading of a text enables readers to gain insights that exceed a cursory reading.

COMPARE To examine two or more objects, ideas, people, etc., in order to note similarities.

CONTRAST To examine two or more objects, ideas, people, etc., in order to show or emphasize differences.

DISTRACTOR Anything that steers a reader away from the text evidence and weakens or misguides analysis.

EVIDENCE Information from the text that a reader uses to prove a position, conclusion, inference, or big idea.

FIX-UP STRATEGIES Common techniques used when meaning is lost.

GENRE A system used to classify types or kinds of writing.

HEADING/SUBHEADING A phrase in larger font or bold-faced print that provides information on the topic of a section of text.

INFERENCE A conclusion that a reader draws about something by using information that is available.

INFORMATIONAL TEXT A type of nonfiction text, such as articles, essays, opinion piece, memoirs, and historical, scientific, technical, or economic accounts, that is written to give facts or inform about a topic.

LITERARY ELEMENTS The component parts found in a whole work of literature.

LITERATURE Imaginary writing, such as poetry, mysteries, myths, creation stories, science fiction, allegories, and other genres, that tells a story.

POETIC TECHNIQUE The elements found in poetry, including figurative language, imagery, personification, rhythm, rhyme, repetition, alliteration, assonance, consonance, onomatopoeia, and layout of text.

SUMMARY A short account of a text that gives the main points, but not all the details.

TEXT FEATURES The variety of tools used to organize text and to give readers more information about the text.

TEXT STRUCTURE The logical arrangement and organization of ideas in a text using sentences, lines, paragraphs, stanzas, sections, etc.

THEME The central message of a text or what the story is really about.

FOR MORE INFORMATION

Council of Chief State School Officers
One Massachusetts Avenue NW, Suite 700
Washington, DC 20001-1431
(202) 336-7000
Website: http://www.ccsso.org
The Common Core State Standards Initiative is a state-led effort coordinated by
the National Governors Association Center for Best Practices (NGA Center)
and the Council of Chief State School Officers (CCSSO). The standards
provide a clear and consistent framework to prepare students for college and
the workforce.

National Association for the Education of Young Children
1313 L Street NW, Suite 500
Washington, DC 20005
(202) 232-8777
Website: http://www.naeyc.org
The National Association for the Education of Young Children is the world's
largest organization working on behalf of young children.

National Education Association
1201 16th Street, NW
Washington, DC 20036-3290
(202) 833-4000
Website: http://www.nea.org
The National Education Association (NEA), the nation's largest professional
employee organization, is committed to advancing the cause of public
education.

National Governors Association
Hall of the States
444 North Capitol Street, Suite 267

Washington, DC 20001-1512

(202) 624-5300

Website: http://www.nga.org

National Parent Teacher Association

12250 North Pitt Street

Alexandria, VA 22314

(703) 518-1200

Website: http://www.pta.org

The National PTA enthusiastically supports the adoption and implementation by all states of the Common Core State Standards. The standards form a solid foundation for high-quality education.

New York State Education Department

89 Washington Avenue

Albany, NY 12234

(518) 474-3852

Website: http://www.engageny.org

EngageNY.org is developed and maintained by the New York State Education Department. This is the official website for current materials and resources related to the implementation of the New York State P-12 Common Core Learning Standards (CCLS).

Partnership for Assessment of Readiness for College and Careers

1400 16th Street NW, Suite 510

Washington, DC 20036

(202) 745-2311

Website: http://www.parcconline.org

The Partnership for Assessment of Readiness for College and Careers (PARCC) is a consortium of eighteen states plus the District of Columbia and the U.S. Virgin Islands working together to develop a common set of K–12 assessments in English and math anchored in what it takes to be ready for college and careers.

U.S. Department of Education
400 Maryland Avenue SW
Washington, DC 20202
(800) 872-5327
Website: http://www.ed.gov
Nearly every state has now adopted the Common Core State Standards. The federal government has supported this state-led effort by helping to ensure that higher standards are being implemented for all students and that educators are being supported in transitioning to new standards.

Websites

Due to the changing nature of Internet links, Rosen Publishing has developed an online list of websites related to the subject of this book. This site is updated regularly. Please use this link to access the list:

http://www.rosenlinks.com/CCRGR/Comp

BIBLIOGRAPHY

Beers, Kylene, and Robert E. Probst. *Notice & Note: Strategies for Close Reading.* Portsmouth, NH: Heinemann, 2013

Cooligan, L. H. *Debating the Issue: Global Warming.* Tarrytown, NY: Marshall Cavendish Benchmark, 2011.

Fountas, Irene C., and Gay Su Pinnell. *Genre Study: Teaching with Fiction and Nonfiction Books.* Portsmouth, NH: Heinemann, 2012

Levin, Judith. *Tattoos and Indigenous People.* New York, NY: Rosen Publishing, 2008.

Nagle, Jeanne. *Tattooing: Why People Get Tattoos and Other Body Art.* New York, NY: Rosen Publishing, 2011.

Robinson, Matthew. *America Debates Global Warming: Crisis or Myth?* New York, NY: Rosen Publishing, 2008.

INDEX

About the Authors

Sandra K. Athans is a National Board Certified practicing classroom teacher with fifteen years of experience teaching reading and writing at the elementary level. She is the author of several teacher-practitioner books on literacy including *Quality Comprehension* and *Fun-tastic Activities for Differentiating Comprehension Instruction*, both published by the International Reading Association. Athans has presented her research at the International Reading Association, the National Council of Teachers of English Conferences, and the New York State Reading Association Conferences. Her contributions have appeared in well-known literacy works including *The Literacy Leadership Handbook* and *Strategic Writing Mini-Lessons.* She is also a children's book writer and specializes in high-interest, photo-informational books published with Millbrook Press, a Division of Lerner Publishing Group.

Athans earned a B.A. in English from the University of Michigan, an M.A. in elementary education from Manhattanville College, and an M.S. in literacy (birth–grade 6) from Le Moyne College. She is also certified to teach secondary English. In addition to teaching in the classroom, she is an adjunct professor at Le Moyne College and provides instruction in graduate-level literacy classes. This spring she was awarded outstanding elementary social studies educator by the Central New York Council for the Social Studies. Athans serves on various ELA leadership networks and collaborates with educators nationwide to address the challenges of the Common Core Standards. The Tips and Tricks series is among several Common Core resources she has authored for Rosen Publishing.

Robin W. Parente is a practicing reading specialist and classroom teacher with over fifteen years of experience teaching reading and writing at the elementary level. She also serves as the elementary ELA coordinator for a medium-sized district in central New York, working with classroom teachers to implement best literacy practices in the classroom. Parente earned a B.S. in elementary education and a M.S. in education/literacy from the State University of New York, College at Oswego. She is a certified reading specialist (PK–12) and elementary classroom teacher and has served on various ELA leadership networks to collaborate with educators to address the challenges of the Common Core Standards. The Tips and Tricks series is among several Common Core resources she has authored for Rosen Publishing.

Photo Credits

Cover © iStockphoto.com/Steve Debenport; pp. 4–5 wizdata/Shutterstock.com; p. 8 michaeljung/Shutterstock.com; p. 14 Rischgitz/Hulton Archive/Getty Images; p. 17 Culture Club/Hulton Archive/Getty Images; p. 22 Universal Images Group/Getty Images; p. 24 Mondadori Portfolio/Hulton Fine Art Collection/Getty Images; p. 27 Print Collector/Hulton Archive/Getty Images; p. 35 Popperfoto/Getty Images; p. 39 Marty Melville/AFP/Getty Images; p. 46 Bloomberg/Getty Images; p. 51 David McNew/Getty Images; icons © iStockphoto/sodafish, © iStockphoto/nipponsan, © iStockphoto/sjhaytov, © iStockphoto/Tantoon Studio, © iStockphoto/Aaltazar.

Designer: Nicole Russo; Editor: Bethany Bryan;
Photo Researcher: Cindy Reiman

WITHDRAWN

32.95   12/10/14

LONGWOOD PUBLIC LIBRARY
800 Middle Country Road
Middle Island, NY 11953
(631) 924-6400
longwoodlibrary.org

LIBRARY HOURS

Monday-Friday	9:30 a.m. - 9:00 p.m.
Saturday	9:30 a.m. - 5:00 p.m.
Sunday (Sept-June)	1:00 p.m. - 5:00 p.m.